YOU CAN
play bass guitar

by Peter Pickow

Copyright © 1998 by Amsco Publications,
A Division of Music Sales Corporation, New York, NY.

Order No. AM 945703
US International Standard Book Number: 0.8256.1655.7
UK International Standard Book Number: 0.7119.6773.3

Exclusive Distributors:
Music Sales Corporation
257 Park Avenue South, New York, NY 10010 USA
Music Sales Limited
8/9 Frith Street, London W1V 5TZ England
Music Sales Pty. Limited
120 Rothschild Street, Rosebery, Sydney, NSW 2018, Australia

Printed in the United States of America by
Vicks Lithograph and Printing

Amsco Publications
New York • London • Sydney

Compact Disc Track Listing

TABLE OF CONTENTS

Introduction

It's true, with a little study and practice, anyone can play bass guitar. This proven bass program will give you the chance to play a variety of popular styles—including rock, pop, blues, jazz, and classical music. This easy, step-by-step method will guide you through all the basics of bass performance and technique. You'll strengthen and develop these important playing skills in exciting performance sessions when you play along with popular hits.

This comprehensive method is easy and fun—and does not rely on tricks and shortcuts that only work for certain songs in certain keys. On the contrary, you can learn to play a variety of music in different keys—and develop all the skills you need to learn hundreds of new songs on your own after you finish the program.

Whether you intend to be a professional bass player or simply wish to play for your community, family, and friends—this book is for you. So, get ready to learn the basics of bass guitar as you play the world's most popular songs.

Holding Your Bass Guitar

You probably will do most of your practicing sitting down. Place the bass on your right thigh. Hold it against your body and let your right forearm rest comfortably on top. Your left elbow should be fairly close to your body.

You will need a strap to play in a standing position. If you don't already have a strap, you can get one at any music store.

Attach the strap to the bass and place it over your left shoulder. While sitting and holding the instrument in its usual position, adjust the strap until it is just taut. When you stand up, the strap will hold the bass in the proper position.

Tuning Your Bass Guitar

Before you begin to practice or play, you should always make sure that your bass is in tune. You tune each string to its correct pitch by turning the appropriate *tuning peg.*

Relative Tuning

If your bass is already pretty well in tune, you can use the *relative tuning* method to tune up.

- Use a left-hand finger to press down on the fourth string (low E) just behind (to the left of) the fifth fret. When you pluck this string, you will hear an A note. This note should sound the same as the third string played *open* (that is, without being fretted by a left-hand finger).
- If the third string (or A string) does not sound in tune, use the tuning peg to loosen it until it sounds lower than the fourth string, fifth fret. Then slowly bring it up to pitch.
- When your A string is in tune, fret it at the fifth fret. This note is D, and should sound the same as the open D, or second, string.
- When your D string is in tune, fret it at the fifth fret. This note is G, and should sound the same as the open G, or first, string.

This diagram summarizes the relative tuning method.

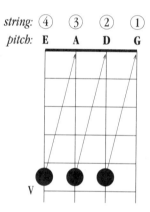

Relative Tuning Method

Tuning by Harmonics

Harmonics are tones produced without actually fretting a string. Instead, just touch the string lightly with a left-hand finger directly above the fret indicated. Strike (pluck) the string with your right-hand index or middle finger and re-move the left-hand finger immediately. The result is a high, bell-like tone. In fact, harmonics are often referred to as *chimes.* The easiest harmonics to sound are those produced by touching the strings at the twelfth fret. Try playing a few of these to get the idea.

Like the relative tuning method, this method can only tell you if your bass is in tune to itself. If you are playing with other people, you will need to tune at least one of your strings to one of the other instruments before applying this method.

- Assuming that your E (fourth) string is in tune, sound the harmonic at the fifth fret. This tone (E) should sound the same as the harmonic on the A (third) string, seventh fret. If the two tones are not perfectly in tune, loosen the A string until it sounds lower, and then slowly bring it up to pitch.
- When your A string is in tune, sound its harmonic at the fifth fret. Compare and match this tone (A) to the harmonic on the D (second) string, seventh fret.
- When your D string is in tune, sound its harmonic at the fifth fret. Compare and match this tone (D) to the harmonic on the G (first) string, seventh fret.

This diagram summarizes tuning by harmonics.

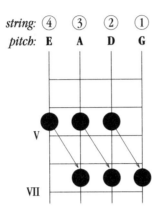

Tuning to a Guitar

The four strings of the bass are tuned to the same pitches as the four lowest strings of the guitar (except that the bass strings sound one octave lower). This makes it relatively easy to get in tune with a guitarist. To make it easier to compare and match the pitch of each string, sound each of your notes as a harmonic at the twelfth fret. When you do this, your strings will sound exactly the same pitches as those of the guitar strings.

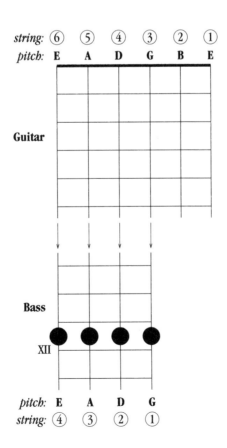

Tuning to a Piano

You can use a tuned piano or electronic keyboard instrument to tune each string of your bass guitar. Here are the notes on the keyboard that correspond to the open strings of the bass. These notes represent the actual sounds of the bass-guitar strings. However, music for bass is written one octave higher than it sounds to make it easier to read.

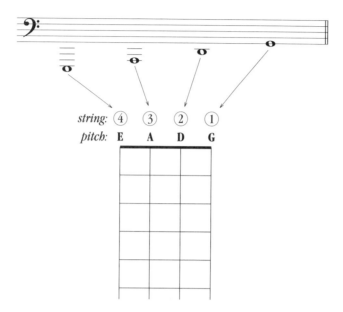

Here again, it may be easier for you to hear these tones accurately if you sound them as harmonics at the twelfth fret. This makes them sound one octave higher. Harmonics also have a purer tone, making the actual pitch more discernible.

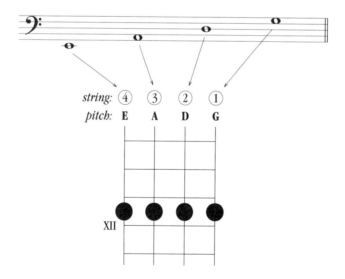

Reading Music and Tablature

The song melodies in this book are written in standard music notation. You can use the "Table of Notes" toward the end of the book to play the melody to any of the songs that may be unfamiliar to you. The accompaniment parts are written in special notation that will make it easy for you to start playing terrific parts right away. Many songs and examples are presented in *tablature,* a well-known system of notation designed specially for guitarists and bass players. This system has a long and venerable history dating back to the lute music of the Renaissance. Our modern tablature system uses a *staff* composed of four lines. Each line represents a string of the bass guitar, with string **1** being the highest, and string **4,** the lowest.

Fretting

In order to *fret* a string, your left-hand fingertip must press it to the fingerboard just behind (to the left of) a fret. Fret numbers placed on lines of bass tablature tell you which fret to play on a given string. (Fret **1** is the one nearest to the tuning pegs.) For instance, this tab tells you to play three different notes on the low E string. Use your left middle finger to press down on the string at the second fret. Then sound this note by plucking the string with your right-hand index finger. Release your middle finger and press down on the first fret with your index finger, and play the second note. Then play the string without fretting, as indicated by the **0** for *open string.*

If you hear buzzing or a muffled tone when you play fretted notes, your fretting finger is probably too close to (or too far away from) the fret. Or it may be that you are just not pressing down hard enough. Here are several things to keep in mind that will help you to get a clear sound on fretted notes.

- **Use your fingertips.** Arch your fingers so that they come straight down on the strings. Imagine you are making an "okay" sign with your thumb and index finger.
- **Keep your thumb in the middle of the back of the neck.** Although it is tempting to let your thumb slide up and peek over the top of the neck, keep it in the middle, just opposite the middle finger. This will help your fingers to stay properly arched.
- **Keep your wrist low and your elbow close to the body.** This will also help you to bring your fingers down accurately and firmly.
- **Avoid tensing your shoulder.** This bad habit will limit your mobility. If your shoulder and arm are not relaxed, it can be difficult to change fret positions smoothly.

Don't worry if fretting notes feels a little uncomfortable at first. It's normal for beginning bass players to get sore fingertips. As you practice, your fingertips will develop calluses, and fretting notes will begin to feel more natural to you.

Reading Rhythms

With tablature to show you where to put your fingers, you now need to know how long to hold each note. First let's look at three different types of note values and their duration in beats. Notice how the notes are distinguished by the presence or absence of a line or *stem*—and by the appearance of the *notehead,* which may be either outlined or filled in. In tablature, the notehead is replaced by a fret number, which may be plain or circled.

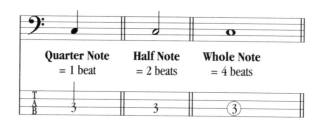

These basic note values form a pattern. The *half note* (which lasts for two beats) is twice the length of the *quarter note* (which lasts for one beat). Similarly, the *whole note* (four beats) is twice the length of the half note (two beats).

A *time signature* at the beginning of a song tells you how many beats there are per *measure* (or *bar*) and what kind of note equals one beat. The most common time signature is 4/4, which is often referred to as *common time* and abbreviated as **C.** The top **4** of 4/4 tells you that there are four beats in each measure. The bottom **4** means that a quarter note gets one beat.

Try playing a few bars of 4/4 time with four quarter-notes per measure. You can use a metronome or just tap your foot to keep the beat even. Count out loud as you use your right index finger to play the notes slowly and evenly on the fourth and third strings. The double barline with two dots at the end of this piece is a *repeat sign,* which tells you to go back to the beginning and play the section over again.

Now take a look at the first phrase of the traditional melody "Jingle Bells," which contains quarter notes, half notes, and whole notes in 4/4. Count each beat aloud as you clap the rhythm of "Jingle Bells"—that is, count out each beat number slowly and evenly, but clap only on the beats that correspond to notes of the melody (these beat numbers appear in boxes).

Playing a Melody

When you play bass guitar in a band, you are the "bottom" of the band. To be a good bass player, especially in rock and country music, you must support the rest of the band by playing the essential and most basic notes of each chord. However, to learn your way around the bass, it's helpful—not to mention, fun—to practice playing melodies. To get started, let's explore some important right-hand techniques.

Picks and Fingers

There are two basic approaches to right-hand technique: fingerstyle and playing with a pick. A well-rounded bass player is able to play in both these styles. We will start out using the right-hand index and middle fingers. Try playing the first string (G) with first your index finger and then your middle finger. Keep these suggestions in mind as you alternate the two fingers slowly and evenly.

- **Use rest strokes.** To execute a *rest stroke,* move your finger straight across the string and let the finger come to rest on the next lower string. Rest strokes ensure evenness of attack and tone and also help your rhythm and time-keeping.
- **Keep your fingers straight.** With each stroke, your finger should move from the knuckle at the base of your finger.
- **Arch your wrist.** This helps you to keep your fingers straight.
- **Keep your fingers perpendicular to the strings.** Also extend your thumb a bit to the left to pull your hand into line.

Now get ready to play the first phrase of "Jingle Bells" with your right-hand index and middle fingers. Start with the index finger, and then alternate as shown (*i*=index, *m*=middle). The tablature will show you the string and fret for each note. The numbers next to the notes in the standard notation tell you which left-hand fingers to use for the fretted notes (**1**=index, **2**=middle, **3**=ring, **4**=pinky). Count each beat as you play.

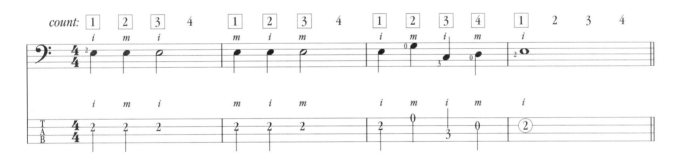

Eighth Notes

Many tunes contain short notes that are worth only one-half of a beat. These notes are called *eighth notes.*

Eighth Note
= 1/2 beat

Eighth notes often occur in groups of two or more. These groups are linked with a bar called a *beam*. Count and clap the rhythm in the second phrase of "Jingle Bells." Remember to count each beat number aloud, but clap only on the beats that appear in boxes. The eighth notes in the second measure are counted with the word "and" between beats.

Now play the full chorus of "Jingle Bells," beginning on the second string. Practice "Jingle Bells" (without counting) until you can play it with confidence at a moderate speed.

Jingle Bells

"Ode to Joy" is another good practice melody. Use all four strings to play this famous theme from Beethoven's Ninth Symphony. Pay attention to the right-hand fingering indications as you skip from the fourth string to the second string in the twelfth measure.

Ode to Joy

Playing a Bassline

So far, you've played two song melodies. In the next section, you'll learn a boogie/rock bassline that you can use to back up hundreds of songs.

Rests and Ties

In the last measure of the "Boogie-Rock Bassline," you will see two kinds of *rests*. The *eighth rest* (ʏ) indicates silence for one-half of a beat. The *quarter rest* (𝄽) indicates silence for one beat. To stop the low E string from ringing through the rests, *damp* it (touch it lightly) with the heel of your right hand.

Another new symbol appearing in the last measure is the curved line connecting the eighth-note E to the final quarter-note E. This curved line is called a *tie,* which indicates that you hold the note through for the combined lengths of the eighth note and quarter note—a total of one-and-a-half beats.

You may want to try playing this bassline with a pick. Most bass players use a heavy or medium pick in the standard teardrop shape. Keep your hand relaxed so that the pick rests on your curled index finger while the thumb holds it in place. Allow the pick to be as flexible in your hand as possible without dropping it. One of the advantages of using a pick is that it makes it easy to play a fast string of notes with alternating *downstrokes* and *upstrokes.* The movement should come mostly from the wrist, but you can put some force behind each stroke by using your forearm a bit also. A downstroke (⊓) is down toward the floor and an upstroke (v) is up toward the ceiling.

Now try the "Boogie-Rock Bassline." If you don't want to use a pick, you can play this whole piece with alternating right-hand index and middle fingers. Use your left index finger (**1**) to play the notes on the second fret and your left ring finger (**3**) for the fourth-fret notes.

Boogie/Rock Bassline

Major Scales

All melodies and basslines are made up of notes taken from *scales*. Learning to play a variety of scales on the bass will help you to be able to come up with your own bassline to any song. Practicing scales is also a great way to learn your way around the fretboard as you build speed and endurance.

For our first scale, let's try C major. It is made up entirely of *natural* notes (no sharps or flats) and so should be easy for you to read. Remember to follow the left-hand fingering indications in the music: **1**=index, **2**=middle, **3**=ring, **4**=pinky, **0**=open string.

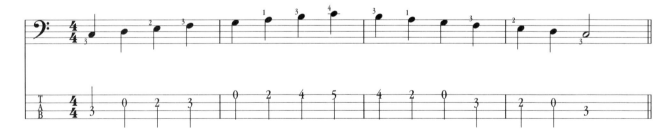

Sound familiar? The C major scale you have just played is in *first position* (first finger, first fret; second finger, second fret; third finger, third fret; and fourth finger, fourth fret) except for the top three notes, for which you have to move up to *second position* (first finger, second fret; second finger, third fret; third finger, fourth fret; fourth finger, fifth fret).

Here is the same C major scale played entirely in second position with no open strings.

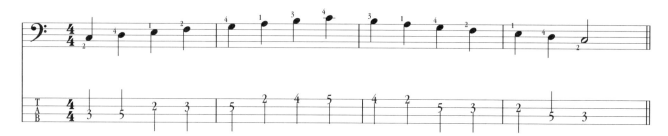

This idea of playing in positions is very important, because if you can play something in one position without using open strings, you can move it anywhere on the neck and play it in any key. For example, let's take the second-position C major scale and slide it up two frets to *fourth position*. Now you will be starting on the note D, and so you will be playing a D major scale.

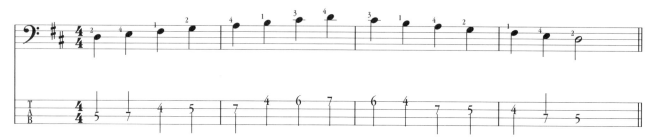

You can see that the relationship of the pitches to one another will remain the same no matter where you start. Take some time to try this scale pattern all up and down the fretboard.

To take this idea of moveable positions one step further, let's play the G major scale.

It feels a lot like the C and D scales under you fingers. The fingering is the same but the strings have been changed. If you move this second-position G scale up to fourth position, it becomes an A major scale.

As with the C scale, you can move this G scale up the neck until you run out of frets, and it will still be the major scale of the note on which you start.

Roots and Fifths

The most important parts of any chord to a bass player are its *root* and its *fifth*. If you know that chords are formed by taking specific notes out of a scale, you can probably guess what a fifth is: the fifth note of the scale. The root of the chord is the first note of the scale. If you look back at the C major scale you played in the last section, you can see that the root is C and the fifth is G.

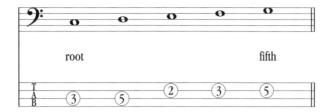

Continuing up the scale you will find another C on top.

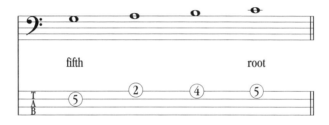

Extending the scale downward from the root discloses another fifth.

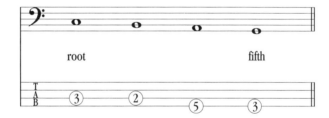

Just like the scale patterns, this pattern of roots and fifths may be moved anywhere on the neck.

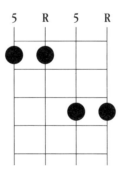

It also follows that the pattern may be moved over a string to produce the root and fifth of a G major scale or chord.

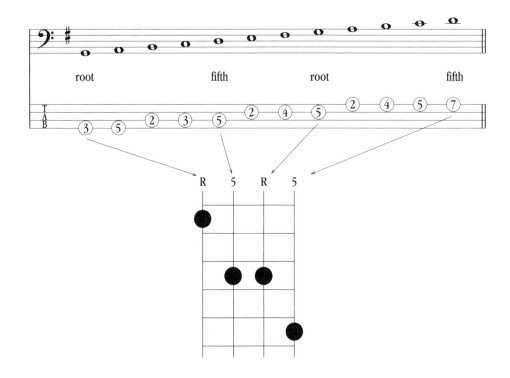

These two positions are the most important anchors that a bass player has. Try these simple basslines to really get a feel for these essential positions.

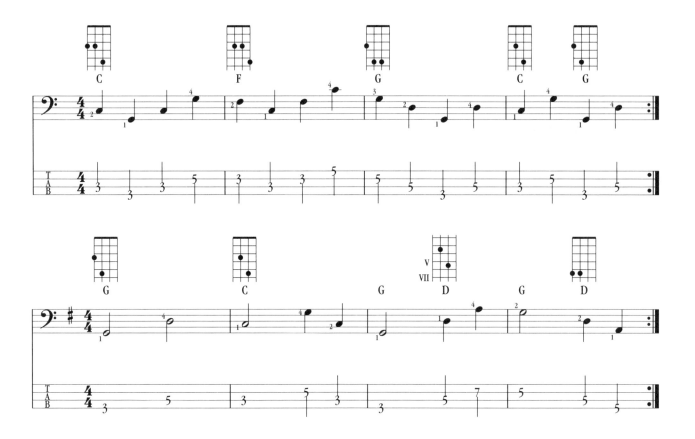

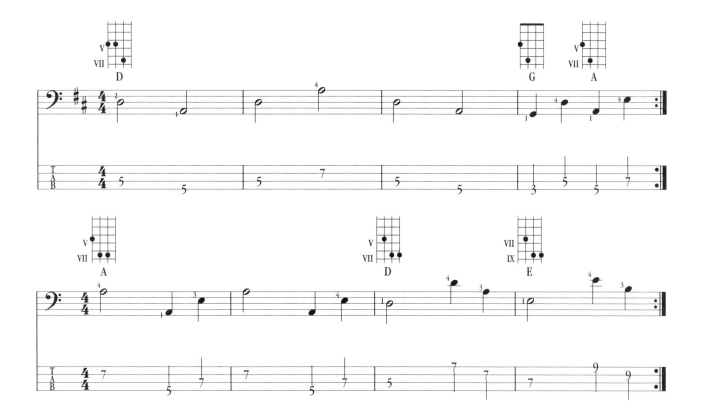

Now here is "Tom Dooley," a traditional American favorite which was a gold-record hit for the Kingston Trio. Play the simple bassline shown, and pay special attention to how the two basic positions are used.

Tom Dooley

Naming Chords by Number

The basslines at the end of the last section are good examples of simple, regular chord progressions. Although each progression uses different chords, the effect is quite similar. This is because within each progression the three chords used bear the same relationship to each other, but each group of three belongs to a different *key*. Because these relationships are so standard, musicians often refer to chords within a key by number. Each set of three chords in the examples above consists of the **I** (one), **IV** (four), and **V** (five) chords of each key.

Key	I	IV	V
C	C	F	G
G	G	C	D
D	D	G	A
A	A	D	E

You can tell from the regular sound of these progressions how important it can be to know the position of the I, IV, and V chords in any key in which you happen to be playing. Here are the fretboard patterns for the roots of the I, IV, and V chords when the root of the I chord is on the third (and first) string.

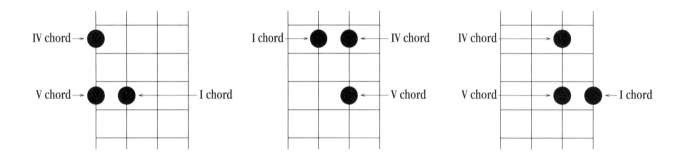

Move these patterns over a string, and you have the patterns of the roots of I, IV, and V chords when the root of the I chord is on the fourth (and second) string.

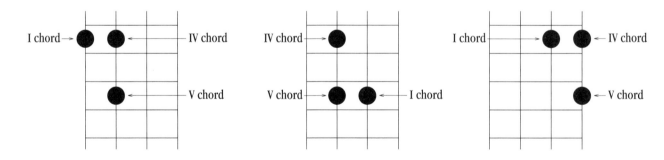

Here is the first of the sample basslines from the last section transposed from the key of C up to the key of E-flat. After you have identified the I-IV-V patterns and how they work, try transposing this example to other keys.

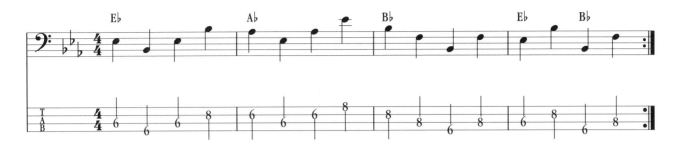

Now let's take the second of the examples and transpose it from G up to B.

Again, try moving this example around to some other positions to really get the feel for the patterns of I, IV, and V chords in different keys.

Fills

In most styles of popular music, the bass and drums play a fairly standardized rhythmic pattern throughout most of the song. Every two or four bars, however, one or both of them will usually vary the pattern a bit to "fill in" or punctuate the overall flow of the tune. These little figures are called *fills*. A fill can either be a simple device to keep rhythm and harmony moving or a dramatic punctuation between phrases or sections of a tune.

Walkups

The simplest fills are *scale runs,* short melodic fragments made up of notes from the major scale. A good example of this type of fill is a *walkup.*

A walkup may be found at the beginning of a tune or, very often, after a *stop* in the middle of a song. It is also a common device for announcing the beginning of a new verse or chorus. Here is a typical root/fifth bassline with a sort of simple, country flavor that uses walkups at the beginning and in the middle. Play it at a moderate tempo, and be careful not to rush the fills.

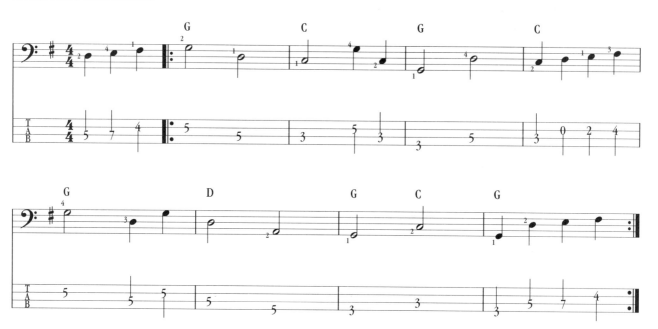

A walkup does not necessarily have to "walk up." Here are a few examples that "walk down" to approach the root of the following chord from above.

Chromatic Fills

Fills are not limited to scale tones. Since the roots of the IV and V chords are both scale steps, moving from one to the other is a prime situation in which to introduce some *chromatic* ideas. This term simply means including notes from outside the scale.

Try these two short bassline examples that use chromatic fills between the IV and V chords.

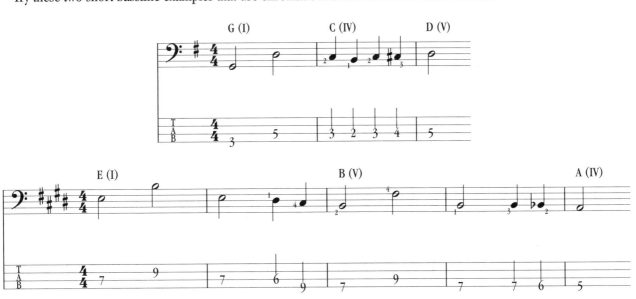

The following arrangement of "Old Joe Clark" makes use of several different types of fills. This old-time hoedown song is based on a square-dance tune—so once you know it well, you should try to play it at a pretty good clip. This arrangement has both a *first ending* and *second ending*. When you get to the end, play the measure bracketed as **1.** Then go back to the point at which you see the inverted repeat sign (the beginning of the third line) and play the section again. This time, skip the measure bracketed as **1** and play the measure bracketed as **2** instead.

Old Joe Clark

Old Joe Clark, he had a house,___ Six - teen sto - ries high,
I went down to Old Joe's house,___ Old Joe was not home,

Ev - ery sto - ry in that house,___ Full of chick - en pie.
I ate all of Old Joe's meat,___ Left Old Joe___ the bone.

Fare thee well,___ Old Joe Clark, Fare thee well,___ I say.

Fare thee well,___ Old Joe Clark, Ain't got long - to stay.
I'm a - go - in' a - way.___

The following arrangement of "Simple Gifts" makes extensive use of fills to connect each chord to the next. In a slow tune such as this, it is very important that you give each note its full value before playing the next note. This is called playing *legato*.

Simple Gifts

Right- and Left-Hand Damping

When practicing or playing, you should always strive to give every note its full value. When you are practicing alone, this *legato* style of playing may sound a bit strange at first. When playing with a band, however, the bass player who leaves gaps between the notes is punching holes in the music. There are special situations where cutting notes short—playing *staccato* as opposed to *legato*—can be used to create an effect.

Damping is a technique that is used to stop a note from ringing. You can damp an open string with either hand by just touching it enough to stop it vibrating. To damp a fretted string, just release the pressure of the left-hand finger fretting the note, but don't lift the finger completely off of the string. Bringing a right-hand finger in contact with a string, either in preparation for a rest stroke on that string or as the completion of a rest stroke on the next higher string, will also effectively damp the ringing string.

If you play the following bassline with rest strokes, you will find that cutting off each note is taken care of by the execution of the next.

In this type of situation, you must take care to give each note its full duration. If you release pressure with the left-hand fretting finger, or bring a right-hand finger into contact with the string, it will stop the note prematurely.

In this next example, you have just the opposite concern. With each subsequent note on a lower or nonadjacent string, you must use left-hand damping to stop each note just as you play the next.

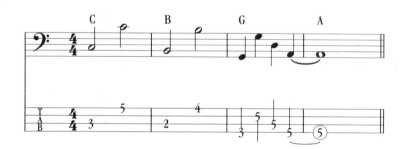

Syncopation

Syncopation is an important rhythmic technique in all kinds of music, especially jazz and rock. Simply speaking, a syncopated bassline is one in which the *offbeats* are accented. Two syncopated patterns are used in the following arrangement of "Sloop *John B.*," a West Indian folk song which became a favorite of the Beach Boys. Their recording of this classic tune stayed on the chart for ten weeks, topping at the third position. The syncopated line helps bring out the Calypso flavor of this lilting melody. Try playing the two bassline patterns used in "Sloop *John B.*" now.

Now play "Sloop *John B.*" at a moderate tempo. Use the first syncopated pattern for the verse and the second pattern for the chorus. A *half rest* appears in the second half of measure 9 of the melody. This rest is worth two beats.

Sloop John B.

Beyond I, IV, and V

As you have learned, the basic chords in any key are the I, IV, and V chords. Naturally, there are plenty of other chords that can show up in more sophisticated progressions. For example, the **II** chord (E7) adds harmonic interest to this rock and roll version of "My Bonnie" with a Motown-style bassline. Notice how this line uses many of the same notes and positions as the bass part to "Sloop *John B*." Here however, the driving beat produces a completely different effect. Once you have mastered the syncopated patterns as shown, try making up a few of your own.

My Bonnie

Chords

Although we seldom play full chords on bass, knowing how chords are constructed can help you to create appropriate basslines in many different styles. Since you already know how to find the fifth of a chord given the root, let's look at what is missing.

Major and Minor Chords

Here are patterns for an A Major chord and an A Minor chord.

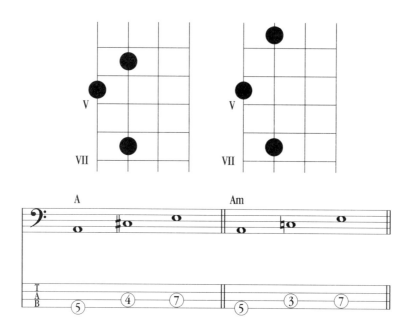

You can see that each chord contains the root and the fifth of the A major scale. The note in between is the *third*. In the major chord it is a *major third* (from the major scale); in the minor chord it is a *minor third* (the major third flatted, or lowered one fret).

You can use these chord patterns to create a bassline like the one below. Notice that the time signature of this example is $\frac{6}{4}$. This time signature is used for slower rock and pop tunes and some blues. Although $\frac{6}{4}$ literally means six beats per measure with one beat to the quarter note, it is most often "felt," or counted, "in two." So, if there were a measure of six quarter-notes, you would feel them as two groups of three with accents on **one** and **four**. (> = accent).

1	2	3	**4**	5	6
>			>		

Putting a heavier accent on beat four produces a *backbeat*.

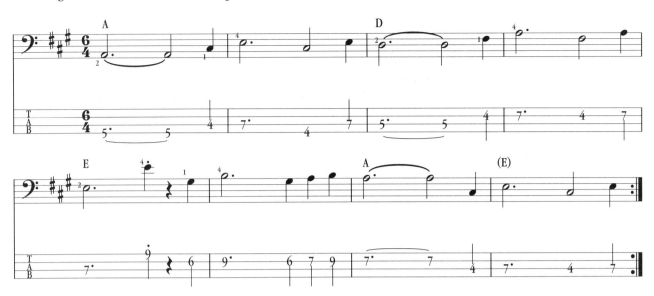

Here's another bassline using major and minor chord patterns. This one is in $\frac{6}{8}$ time, which is felt "in two" like $\frac{6}{4}$. In $\frac{6}{8}$ time, each beat consists of three eighth-notes and the backbeat accent is usually not as strong as in $\frac{6}{4}$ time. The typical $\frac{6}{8}$ rhythm is referred to as a *shuffle rhythm*.

Sixth and Seventh Chords

Adding a *sixth* to the simple three-note chord pattern gives us familiar basslines like these.

The first of these patterns is a standard *walking bass.* Adding a *seventh* to this pattern makes it even more interesting.

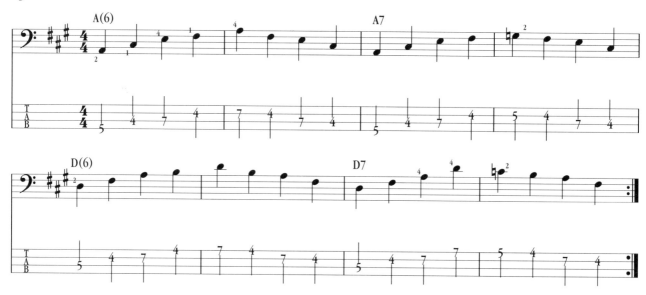

If you play the major-scale pattern and count up to seven, you will find that the note that we have just added is different from the seventh note of the scale. The seventh in a seventh chord is flatted compared to the seventh in the major scale of the same root. This is because the seventh in a seventh chord (like A7 or E♭7) is derived from the seventh note above the V chord. This is why you will sometimes hear them referred to *dominant seventh* chords (another name for the V chord is the *dominant*).

It is not necessary to understand theoretically why this is so; what is important is to understand the moveable chord patterns and be able to apply them. Here is a chart of several patterns for seventh and minor seventh chords including the sixth. A series of notes outlining a chord as these do is sometimes called an *arpeggio*. Notice how the same series of notes can be played in more than one position.

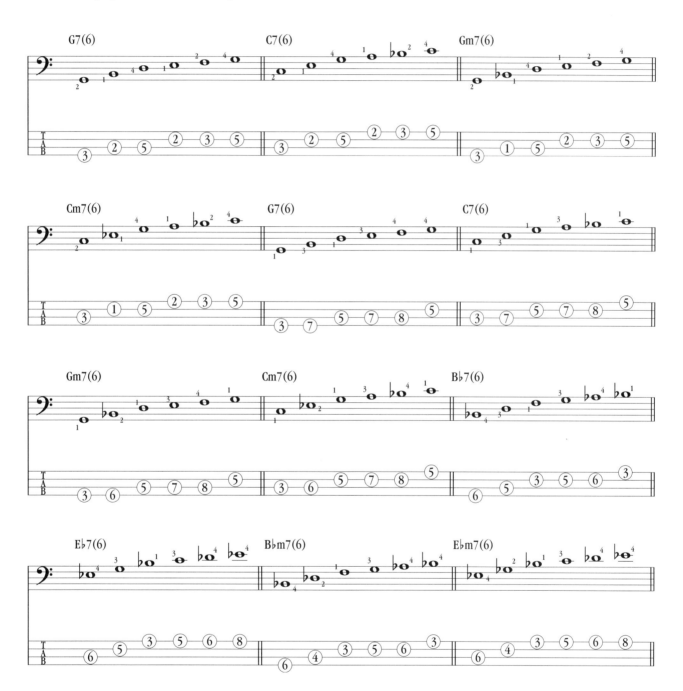

Slides, Hammerons, and Pulloffs

Before we play another tune, let's take a look at some special techniques that can help you to add expression and color to your bass playing.

A *slide* is left-hand technique that you can use to dress up a song. Take a look at the slide found in the last two measures of the verse of "Good Morning Blues." These measures form a *turnaround* lick that you can play at the end of most any blues song. The straight line before the first note of the turnaround tells you to slide up to that note from one or two frets below. Fret the second string with your third finger at the fifth fret. Play the note and quickly slide your third finger along the string up to the seventh fret to sound the written note. Then play the rest of the turnaround as written.

A slide can also be used between two notes. In this case the line would connect the two noteheads in the music and the two numbers in the tablature. There is a slide like this in the last two measures of the solo section. To play this slide, you play the first note and then, without plucking the string again, slide your left-hand finger up or down to the second note. The trick with either type of slide is to arrive at the final pitch exactly in time.

A *hammeron* is a left-hand technique you can use to add polish and variety to a bassline. Like a slide, this technique also involves producing a tone without picking the string with the right hand. The exercise below features hammerons on the fourth and third strings. You'll use a similar riff later when you play the song "Good Morning Blues." The curved line that connects the first two notes is a *slur*. This indicates that you should play the second note as a hammeron.

To begin, fret the fourth string at the fourth fret with your left-hand first finger. Play this note, then bring your left-hand second finger down onto the string to sound the fifth-fret note.

You can also hammer on from an open-string note. Try this exercise to get the feel of this type of hammeron. Notice how a hammeron may be combined with a slide in the second measure.

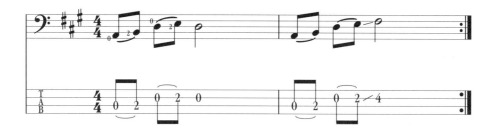

Another left-hand technique is the *pulloff,* which is the opposite of a hammeron. Fret an F♯ note on the second string, fourth fret using your third finger. Also place your left-hand first finger on the second string, second fret. Play the F♯ note, then pluck the string with your left-hand third finger to sound the second-fret note. The symbol for a pulloff is a slur—the same as for a hammeron: You know that this is a pulloff because it is going from one note to a lower note—a hammeron must go from one note to a higher note. You can also pull off to an open-string note. This example has both types of pulloffs.

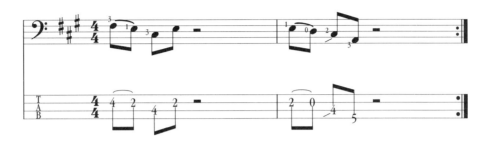

To finish off this section, let's apply some walking bass patterns using sixths and sevenths to the great blues classic "Good Morning Blues."

The melody of this traditional blues features *dotted quarter notes* and *dotted half notes.* A dot after a note increases the note's value by one-half. This means that a dotted quarter note is held for one-and-one-half beats—and a dotted half note is held for three beats.

Watch for a few slides, hammerons, and pulloffs in this bassline (and note how they serve to make the phrasing of the line smooth and bluesy).

Good Morning Blues

Well, I'm do-ing' all right,___ good morn-ing, how are you?___

Sax solo

Pentatonic Scales

A *pentatonic scale* is made up of five notes. There are hundreds of pentatonic scales possible, but only two are commonly used in popular music. The first is conveniently outlined by one of the most famous basslines of all time: the opening bars of Smokey Robinson's "My Girl."

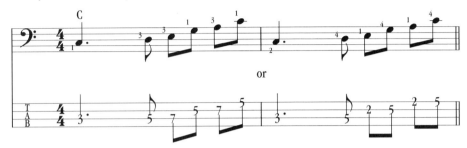

Comparing this five-note scale with the major scale shows it to be made up of the first, second, third, fifth, and sixth degrees.

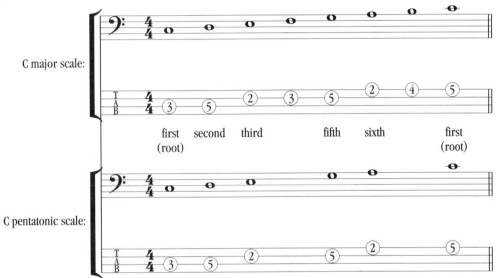

Another way to think of this *major pentatonic scale* is as a major sixth arpeggio with one extra note, the second. Because of this, there is not a whole lot new to say about using the major pentatonic scale to create lines. However, it can be very useful for creating fills like these.

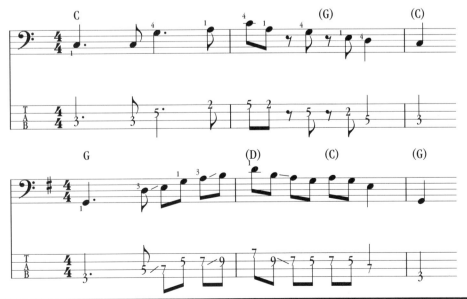

As long as they sound good, and make sense melodically, pentatonic fills will not clash with I, IV, or V chords. In fact, pentatonic lines like the ones above may be played against a variety of different chord progressions. Here is another fill which fits several alternative chord progressions.

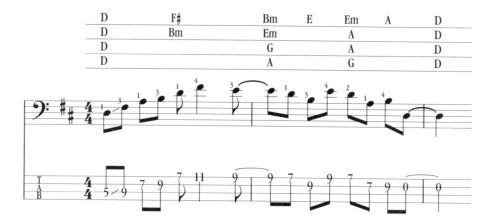

Now let's look at this pentatonic scale from a different slant. If we start on the fifth note of this scale, considering it the root of a new scale, we get a *minor pentatonic scale.*

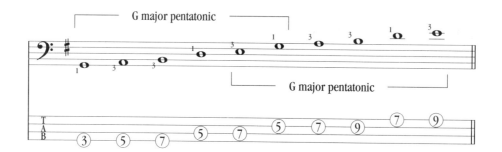

This scale is often called a *blues scale* because, compared to a major scale, it has a flatted third and flatted seventh, which are characteristic *blue notes.* The blues scale is very useful when creating bass parts for blues, rock, or any other kind of pop music. It is also handy for injecting a fleeting bluesy feel into an otherwise major-sounding song. You will get some practice with these minor pentatonic scales later in the "Blues" section of this book.

To sum up, here are some common moveable positions for major pentatonic scales. Study the fretboard diagrams to discover and learn the three basic patterns on which all of these scales are based.

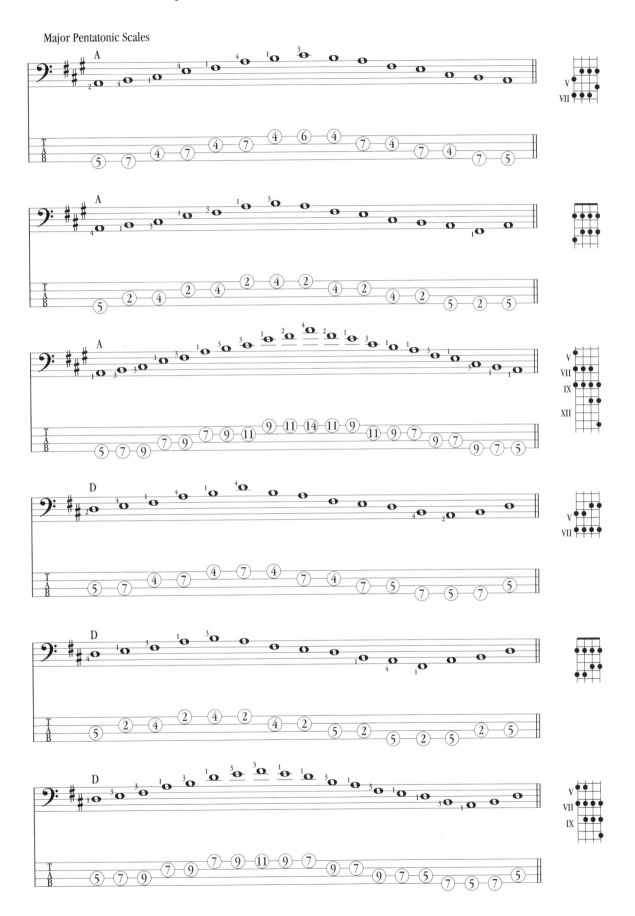

Major Pentatonic Scales

Remember that each one of these patterns also serves as a blues scale; just start on the fifth note of the scale. Here is how this works with the first three fingering patterns from above.

Minor Pentatonic (Blues) Scales

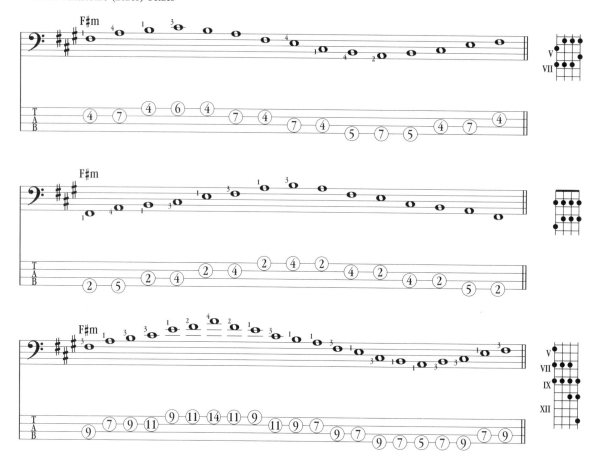

Now you're ready to play "Amazing Grace" in the key of G major. This beloved hymn was written in the late 1700s by John Newton, a reformed slave-trader who saw the light and became a minister. As a tribute to the lasting popularity of this song, Judy Collins made it a top-40 hit in 1971. The following year, the Royal Scots Dragoon Guards of Scotland's armored regiment recorded a bagpipe band version of the tune that put it back on the pop charts. Bill Moyers recently chose this meaningful song as the subject of a documentary special, featuring Jean Ritchie, Judy Collins, and Johnny Cash.

"Amazing Grace" is written in $\frac{3}{4}$ time, with three beats to a measure and one beat per quarter note.

There is also a new rhythmic notation in the bass part: the *triplet*. When you see three eighth-notes beamed together with a *3* over the beam, it means to play the three notes evenly in the space of one beat. Play this exercise which starts out in quarter notes and goes to eighth-note triplets. Count out loud and keep a steady beat as you play.

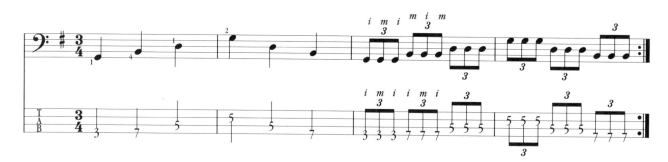

Notice how the bass part of "Amazing Grace" uses several positions of the G major pentatonic scale (and even a bit of the G blues scale). This lends a real gospel feel to the whole arrangement.

Amazing Grace

Developing Your Repertoire

Now that you've got the fundamentals of bass playing under your belt, you're ready to start exploring different styles of music and learning how the bass fits in. As an important part of a band's rhythm section, the bass player plays a crucial role in setting the feel of the music.

In the sections that follow, you'll find bass parts for hit songs in several musical styles—blues, rock, pop, jazz, and classical. As you play the songs that follow, you'll use skills you learned in previous sections. You will also learn new bass techniques that will add style to your playing. Even if you have a special interest in only one or two of these types of music—you'll benefit from playing the songs in each section.

The Blues

The blues was born in the American South. It evolved from the work songs written by African-American slaves before the Civil War—and so bears the influence of African rhythms and tonality. The blues is known for its power to evoke the listener's emotions—because its lyric often tells a personal story of troubles and longing. The plaintive melody and harmony of the blues, coupled with its strong and simple rhythm, make it a universally appealing musical form.

Frankie and Johnny

"Frankie and Johnny" is perhaps the most famous blues of all time. This stark tale of love and murder was recorded by many great blues artists—and was a signature tune for Mae West. As a testament to this song's versatility, R&B singer/songwriter Brook Benton put it on the charts for four weeks in 1961; soul singer Sam Cooke put it on the charts for seven weeks in 1963; and Elvis Presley, the King of Rock and Roll, made it a hit once again for five weeks in 1966.

The rhythm of "Frankie and Johnny" is what is known as a *shuffle rhythm.* This means that the first eighth note in each group of two is held for a slightly longer time than the second. This gives a bouncy blues feel to both melody and accompaniment. The way to get this feeling into your playing is to think of each quarter-note beat as being divided into three. To produce the typical shuffle rhythm, you play only the first and third note in each eighth-note triplet. Try this rhythm with this simple blues bassline.

The bass part for "Frankie and Johnny" is mainly made up of notes from the E minor pentatonic scale, or E blues scale. Here is the basic scale position for you to practice.

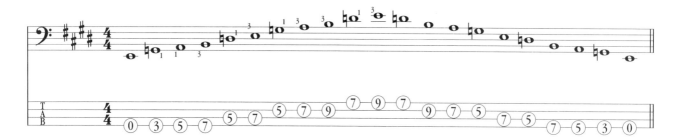

Since the shuffle rhythm is continued throughout the entire song, it is cleaner to write the part out in eighth notes and place the following marking at the top of the piece.

In the last two measures of the verse to "Frankie and Johnny," you will find a classic blues *turnaround* progression that calls for a chromatic walkup. After the second time through, the tag ending gives you some room to "stretch out" and play a bluesy ending fill.

Frankie and Johnny

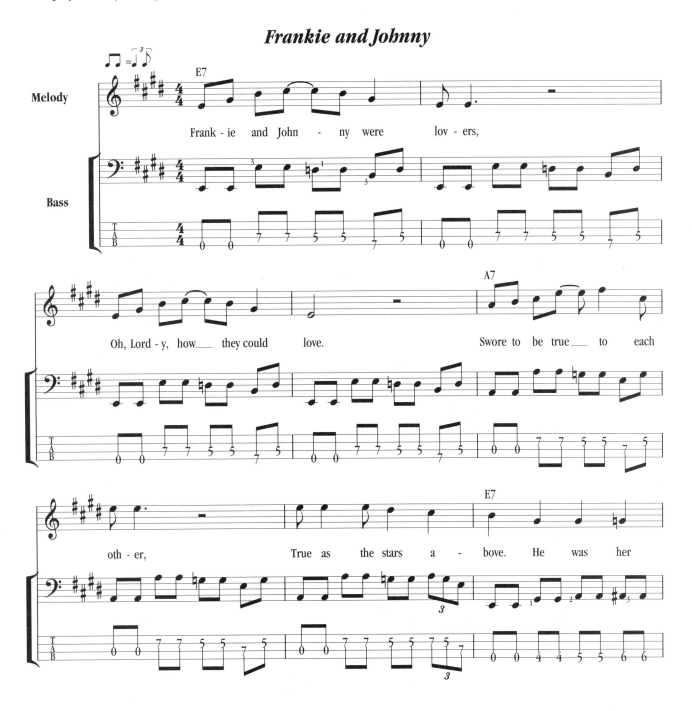

C.C. Rider

"C.C. Rider" is an all-time favorite blues and rock hit that has been performed by a wide range of artists. Ma Rainey brought this tune to position fourteen on the charts in 1925. In 1957, rhythm and blues singer Chuck Willis had a career-making hit with this song—and inspired the dance craze called "The Stroll." In 1963, rhythm and blues singer LaVern Baker recorded her hit version of this tune ("See See Rider"). The magic had still not worn off this terrific rhythm number—for Eric Burdon & the Animals made "See See Rider" a hit once again for seven weeks in 1966.

The basic feel of this arrangement of "C.C. Rider" is what is known as a *Memphis shuffle,* which uses straight eighth notes. The bassline, for the most part, emphasizes the roots of the chords. However, there are plenty of quick fills derived from both the major and minor pentatonic scales.

C.C. Rider

you   have   done,_____   Well, you
made   me   blue,_____   Well, you

made   me   love you,   now   your   love   is   gone._____
made   me   love you,   now   I'm   in   a   stew._____

1.   C7   C#7 D7   2.   F7   F#7 G7

Rock

Rock and roll emerged in the 1950s as "rockabilly" music—a blending of hillbilly-style country music and the driving beat of Black rhythm & blues. Rock's pioneers include Bill Haley, Carl Perkins, Chuck Berry, Elvis Presley, Jerry Lee Lewis, and Little Richard. By the late 1950s, rock and roll was no longer a novelty, but had entered the pop mainstream—with millions of avid fans in American and Europe. In the 1960s, the popularity of rock music was brought to a new peak with the advent of British rock groups, beginning with the Beatles. Other British groups, like the Who and the Rolling Stones, followed soon after. Lots of different rock forms have evolved over the years, including acid rock, glitter rock, southern rock, and heavy metal—but the one thing that all of these forms have in common is that they all depend on the sound of guitar, bass, and drums.

In this section, you'll get to play two classic rock uptunes—hits for Cream and Los Lobos. As you perform each of these tunes, you'll see the close relationship between rock and its parent forms—blues and rhythm & blues.

La Bamba

Latin rock and roll star Ritchie Valens had a hit with "La Bamba" in 1959. The movie based on his life, *La Bamba,* was released in 1987—with music by the Latin-American rock quintet Los Lobos. Their version of this terrific Latin tune held the number one position on the charts for three weeks. The simple I-IV-V chord progression of "La Bamba" has been used for countless rock songs over the years; in fact, you can use the following arrangement to play songs such as "Twist and Shout," "Good Lovin'," and "Do You Love Me."

This bassline also contains a new playing technique. *Damped notes* are indicated by an *x* in place of a notehead. To play a damped note, muffle the string completely with a left-hand finger as you pick it with your right. This produces a percussive effect that can really move a tune along.

To break it up a bit, you'll find several patterns in different positions throughout the arrangement. Once you are familiar with them all, you can mix and match them as you please. Just remember that the part you play must provide a solid foundation for the rest of the band.

La Bamba

*N.C. = no chord

Crossroads

"Crossroads" is a traditional blues tune that Cream turned into a rock and roll hit in 1969. Originally entitled "Crossroad Blues," this song was a favorite of blues master Robert Johnson. Here's a blues-rock version of "Crossroads" that brings out its driving beat. In the introduction, you get to play a *bass/guitar hook* that is similar to the one that Jack Bruce and Eric Clapton played in Cream's version. A bass/guitar hook is simply a recurring riff played together in octaves by the guitarist and bass player in a band. This riff is made up of notes taken from an A blues scale.

The notation of this riff includes a new type of note called a *sixteenth note.* The time value of a sixteenth note is half that of an eighth note, or one-quarter of a quarter note. When you count a measure of eighth notes, you say, "One and, two and, three and, four and." When you count sixteenth notes, you need two extra syllables per beat, so you say, "One-ee-and-ah, two-ee-and-ah, three-ee-and-ah, four-ee-and-ah." Count and play this simple sixteenth-note example.

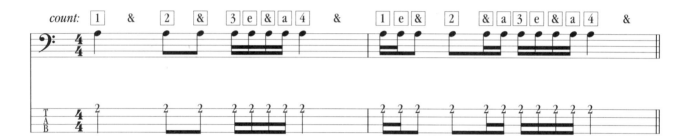

Now try playing the "Crossroads" signature riff. Count out loud as indicated until you can play it smoothly and solidly.

After the four-measure introduction, this arrangement has you playing an eighth-note pattern under the verse. This pattern alternates with the riff until measure 20, in which you get to play a bluesy pulloff fill to lead into the guitar solo. Under the solo, you can play a variation on the eighth-note pattern that's a bit more open and syncopated. The third time through has you playing a busier example of a straight-eighth rock bassline. All of the bassline patterns in this tune contain standard rock bass riffs that may be used in countless rock songs. Try coming up with your own variations as you play this immortal rock song.

Crossroads

Lord to have mer - cy, save me if____ you please.

Pop

Generally speaking, any song or instrumental piece that enjoys wide commercial popularity is considered "pop" music—and the relative success of a pop song is measured by its rank on the pop charts. Contemporary pop and rock musics developed during the 1950s. Early pop music took several forms: there were "doo-wop" groups (like the Marcels and the Five Satins); close-harmony vocal ensembles (like the Supremes and Shirelles); and close-harmony groups doing "surf" music (notably, the Beach Boys and Jan and Dean).

Throughout the sixties and seventies, pop drew more and more influence from rock music—and today, many pop chart hits are actually rock, pop-rock, or "soft rock" music. The music of pop artists like Prince, Madonna, and Michael Jackson combines the harmonious and bright qualities of pop music with the driving beat, bold instrumentation, and special effects of rock music. Today's pop-rock hits are usually dance tunes—and feature strong and evocative rhythms. In this section, you'll focus on hits of the classic pop period as you play the music of Cat Stevens and Elvis Presley.

Morning Has Broken

"Morning Has Broken" is a traditional hymn that captured the attention of Cat Stevens. In 1972, his hit recording of this beautiful tune stayed on the pop charts for eleven weeks, peaking at position six. In this simple arrangement, be sure to play the bassline *legato;* that is, give every note its full value. Notice how notes other than the roots of the chords are used to make the bassline more melodic, almost like a countermelody in places. Some of these moves are implied in the chord changes through the use of *slash chords. F/C* means "F chord with a C note in the bass," *G/B* means "G chord with a B note in the bass," and *Em7/B* means "E minor seven chord with a B note in the bass." Whenever you see these types of chord symbols in a piece of music that you are working on, you should try to come up with a bassline that makes use of these alternative notes.

Morning Has Broken

Morn - ing has brok - en like the first morn - ing.

Black - bird has spok - en like the first bird.

Praise for the sing - ing, praise for the morn -

Fine

Aura Lee (Love Me Tender)

"Aura Lee" (composed by George R. Poulton) has long been considered one of America's most popular love melodies—and it enjoyed a smash revival when Elvis Presley recorded it as "Love Me Tender." This chart-busting hit was the title song for Elvis's first movie—and stayed in the number one position on the charts for five weeks. This popular tune made it back on the charts when Richard Chamberlain recorded it in 1962—and again, as recorded by Percy Sledge in 1967.

The bass part to this arrangement uses a technique called *double-stops*. All this means is that you play two notes at once. Double-stops may be used to imply chords or to play a moving line over a stationary note, called a *pedal tone*. Here are all of the double-stops used in "Aura Lee" for you to practice. Play the lower notes with your right-hand thumb and the upper notes with you index or middle finger.

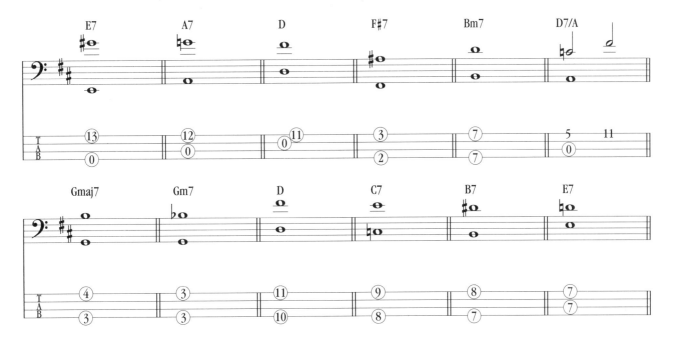

Once you are familiar with these double-stops, play "Aura Lee." When you play the twelfth-fret harmonic in the last measure of this arrangement, let it ring out along with the double-stop notes.

Aura Lee

Jazz

Most music historians agree that jazz is a direct descendant of ragtime and the blues. Like the blues, ragtime emerged from the traditional Black-American folk music of the nineteenth century. Ragtime's inventors are thought to be traveling minstrels who combined elements of Euro-American folk dance and fiddle music with syncopated African rhythms to create a new distinctive musical genre. Ragtime music was characterized by a syncopated melody played with a steady, marchlike harmony part.

Jazz first became popular in the New Orleans area at the turn of the century. This early jazz is often termed *New Orleans jazz*. Like the blues, once jazz spread to other urban centers around the country, it took on new forms. Dixieland and Harlem style jazz added some sophistication to the basic sound—and explored the potential of different instruments in the jazz band. In the 1920s, jazz entered the mainstream of popular song and made its debut on the Broadway stage. Since jazz is largely an instrumental form, musicians found that many older songs could be "jazzed up" to enjoy successful revivals. If a song got played enough by jazz musicians, it became known as a *jazz standard*.

Through the years, jazz has claimed many popular songs, folk tunes, and blues songs for its own. These jazz standards include traditional songs like "A Tisket, a Tasket" and "Frankie and Johnny," as well as commercial hits like "Tea for Two" and "Alexander's Ragtime Band." In fact, most of the songs written by jazz-influenced composers such as Irving Berlin, George Gershwin, and Jerome Kern were reinterpreted by jazz musicians as standard pieces in their performance repertoire.

A Tisket, a Tasket

Ella Fitzgerald is perhaps the greatest jazz singer of all time. After winning the Harlem Amateur Hour in 1934, she created a popular sensation with her jazzy rendition of "A Tisket, a Tasket." Before you play an arrangement of this jazz classic, take some time to learn about a typical harmonic device common to many jazz tunes.

Jazz tunes can present a challenge to the bass player because their chord progressions are often quite complex, with changes coming two or more to the measure. This is a real problem on fast tunes when you want to play a walking bassline. One thing that can save you is to learn to recognize the ubiquitous *II V I progression*.

The II V I progression shows up in every kind of music, but in jazz it seems to have been elevated to a kind of religion. The trick to playing a walking line through a set of changes like this is to be aware of them ahead of time so that you can make up your line from the major scale of the I chord. For instance, here is a fragment of a typical jazz tune.

Notice how this sample bassline follows the temporary changes of key implied by each II V I sequence.

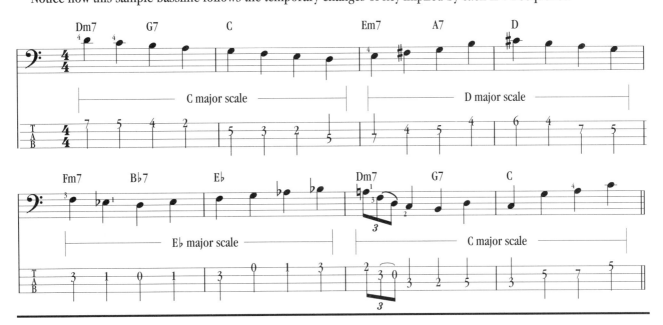

The II V I progression works because the II is the V of the V chord, and so it has the same strong pull toward the V that the V has toward the I. Taking this one step further, we can add the V of the II chord, the VI chord, in front to get a VI II V I progression. Here is a bassline that follows the chord progression to part of a well-known jazz standard with all of the II V I and VI II V I progressions, and the scales that they imply, identified.

A common device in playing II V I progressions is to flat the fifth of some of the chords. Since the fifth of the V chord is always one whole-step (two frets) above the root of the I chord, flatting the fifth so that it is only a half step (one fret) away makes for a very smooth transition from V to I. The same holds true for II to V and for VI to II. Here are the first few bars of the last example using flatted fifths.

The following arrangement of "A Tisket, a Tasket" makes use of the II V I progression in G: Am7 D7 G. The bassline uses flatted fifths as it walks through the chord changes. See if you can spot the points at which the bassline implies the VI chord (E7) before the II V I change.

A Tisket, a Tasket

Jazzy Show Tune

The chord progression to this typical show tune will give you even more practice in playing through VI II V I changes. In fact, this song goes one step further and places the V of the VI chord in front of the sequence to produce a III VI II V I progression (E7 A7 D7 G7 C, in the key of C). There are plenty of scale-step and chromatic walkups and walkdowns throughout the verse sections.

In the bridge—which is an extended III VI II V I sequence—the bass part goes into high gear with a jazzy walking line. The last chord in this section is a G7+. The **+** means that the chord is *augmented;* that is, it contains a sharped fifth (D#). The easiest way to play over an augmented chord is to use notes from the *whole-tone scale.* Here is a G whole-tone scale for you to practice.

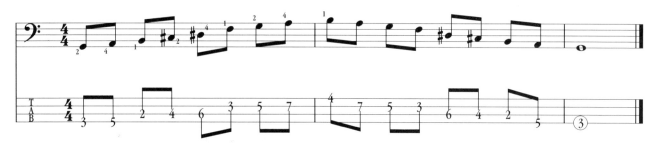

The end of the last verse section moves to a VI chord (A7) to lead you into a typical jazz *tag ending.* Notice how the piano and bass play the melodic signature riff together in the last two measures.

Classical

Technically speaking, classical music is any serious music composed between 1750 and 1820. This term is also commonly applied to music of a serious nature composed in any period—from the late Renaissance to the present. Although there aren't many classical compositions that have a part for electric bass, its close cousin, the acoustic *double bass,* is an important voice in many orchestral works. The double bass is tuned the same as your bass guitar, but it has no frets and is usually played with a bow.

Pomp and Circumstance

"Pomp and Circumstance" (also known as "The Graduation Song") was written by Edward Elgar for the coronation of King Edward VII in 1901. The title is taken from William Shakespeare's *Othello,* Act III, Scene 3. This stately classical piece is best known as the processional music played at graduation ceremonies throughout the world.

 To give you a taste of playing a classical bassline, try reading through this arrangement of "Pomp and Circumstance" now. As always, give every note its full value, and make sure that each note receives equal stress to preserve the stately, dignified feel of the piece. Notice that the chord progression makes use of slash chords and VI II V I sequences just like many pop and jazz tunes. Pay careful attention to the left-hand fingering on the octave jumps, which occur throughout the part.

Pomp and Circumstance

Further Study

Congratulations! You have completed a comprehensive course in bass guitar that will provide a broad foundation for your continued development and personal playing style. The "Table of Notes" that follows will provide you with the key to hours of further study. Use this table to explore reading and playing the basslines and melodies of your favorite songs, as well as ones that are unfamiliar to you. You'll find hours of enjoyment reading through sheet music and song collections as you strengthen these important reading skills.

You may also wish to pursue an in-depth study of chord forms and structure, as is provided in any good music-theory textbook. This further study is especially advisable for those who wish to compose or arrange music. A basic understanding of the more advanced theoretical aspects of written music can only serve to enhance your bass-playing abilities. (Naturally, a well-recommended bass teacher would also greatly enhance your self-study program.) However, at this point, you have all the facts you need to continue your development as a knowledgeable and competent bass player—and the music store and music library will provide you with many new doorways to a lifetime of playing enjoyment.

Table of Notes

In this table, the standard notation contains two sets of notes. The bass staff shows you how the notes appear when you are reading music written for the bass. This line is in *bass clef* (𝄢). The small music staff above the bass staff shows the notes in *treble clef* (𝄞) an octave above the bass-clef notes. You can use this line to help you figure out music found in songbooks, guitar books, and other sources that are not notated for bass.

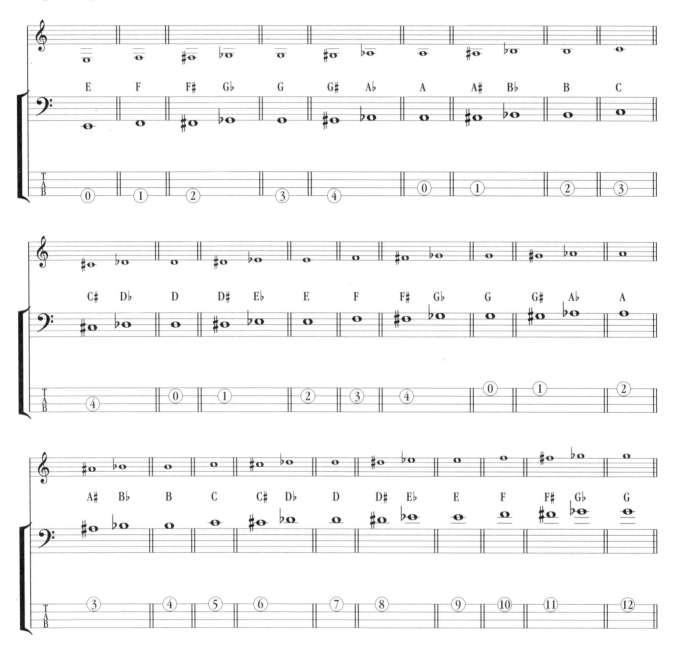